MY SUMMER DIARY

19____

May **21** to September **9**
Plus 20 pages of special fill-ins.

SCHOLASTIC INC.
New York Toronto London Auckland Sydney

Telephone Numbers

Name _____

Telephone Number _____

Name _____

Telephone Number _____

Name _____

Telephone Number _____

Name _____

Telephone Number _____

Name _____

Telephone Number _____

Name _____

Telephone Number _____

Name _____

Telephone Number _____

ISBN 0-590-40114-9

25   5/9

Printed in the U.S.A.   40

Personal Facts

Name _____

Address _____

_____

Telephone Number _____

Age _____

Birthdate _____

Place of Birth _____

Nickname _____

Height _____

Weight _____

Color of Hair _____

Color of Eyes _____

MAY

21

22

23

24

25

26

28

29

30 MEMORIAL DAY

31

Family Affair

Father's Name _____

Mother's Name _____

Brother's(s') Name(s) _____

_____

Sister's(s') Name(s) _____

_____

I have _____ cousins. Their names are

_____

_____

Pet's(s') Name(s) _____

_____

What I like to do most with my family in

summer is _____

_____

_____

_____.

JUNE

1

2

3

4

5

6

7

8

9

10

11

12

13

14

15

16

17

18

19

20

21

22

23

24

25

26

27

28

29

30

School's Out!

The last day of school was _____.

I used to be in _____ grade. My teacher
used to be _____.

On the last day of school we _____
_____.

The thing about school I'm really going to
miss is _____.

The funniest thing that happened at school
last year was _____
_____ .

The worst thing that happened to me at
school was _____
_____ .

My best subject is _____.

My worst subject is _____.

JULY

1

2

3

THE 4th!

8

9

10

11

12

13

14

15

16

20

21

22

26

27

28

29

30

31

Friendship

My summer friends are _____

_____.

When I get together with my friends we like

to _____

_____.

Our favorite place to hang out is _____

_____.

My funniest friend is _____.

The friend I tell all my secrets to is _____

_____.

The friend I've known the longest is _____

_____. We've known

each other since _____.

The new friends I've made this summer are

_____.

Summer Birthdays

Name _____

Birthday _____

Name _____

Birthday _____

Name _____

Birthday _____

Name _____

Birthday _____

The best summer birthday party I ever went

to was _____

_____.

My favorite place to go on my birthday is

_____.

Time Out!

The sport I like most is _____.

In summer I like (circle):

baseball	swimming	tennis
softball	boating	biking
basketball	fishing	horseback riding
soccer	volleyball	other _____

The farthest I ever rode my bike was _____

_____. It took me _____.

(hours, minutes)

The best place I know to go swimming is

_____.

I went fishing this summer at _____

(place)

_____ with _____.

We caught _____ fish!

Favorite Summer Sounds

Song _____

Singer (male) _____

Singer (female) _____

Group _____

Album _____

Video _____

Radio Station _____

I like listening to music most when I'm _____

_____.

My vote for best songs this summer:

#1 _____

by _____

#2 _____

by _____

#3 _____

by _____

Campin' Out

I went to Camp _____

in _____. Camp lasted

_____. We slept in _____

_____ and the food

was _____.

My counselor was _____.

I learned to _____.

I really liked camp because _____

_____.

The worst part about camp was _____

_____.

New friends I met at camp:

Name _____

Hometown _____

Name _____

Hometown _____

Name _____

Hometown _____

Name _____

Hometown _____

Bookshelf

My favorite place to read is _____

_____.

I get books from (circle):

library   friend   bookstore   gifts

Other _____

Books I read this summer

Title _____ Liked Didn't
                                          Like
Author _____

Title _____ Liked Didn't
                                          Like
Author _____

Title _____ Liked Didn't
                                          Like
Author _____

Title _____ Liked Didn't
                                          Like
Author _____

Title _____ Liked Didn't
                                          Like
Author _____

Summer Bummers

It's a real bummer when it rains! But on rainy days, I like to _____

_____.

My favorite rainy-day TV show is _____

_____.

The game I like to play most when it rains

_____.

This summer, I got (circle):

poison ivy   swimmer's ear
a broken _____   sniffles & sneezes
sunburn   a sore throat
scrapes & bruises   nothing!
stitches   other _____

The worst thing that happened this summer

was _____

_____.

At the Movies

The best movie I ever saw was _____

_____.

My favorite actor is _____.

My favorite actress is _____.

The person I like to go to the movies with most

is _____.

This summer I saw _____ movies!

Title _____

Title _____

Title _____

Title _____

Title _____

Title _____

Title _____

Title _____

Title _____

Family Vacation

This summer we went to _____

_____ for _____.
                                               (days, weeks)

We: drove flew rode a train took a bus
went by boat other_____.

It took us _____ to get there.
                         (hours, days)

We left on _____ and got back
                     (date)

_____.
                   (date)

The places we visited were _____

_____.

The best part about the trip was _____

_____

_____.

Next year I hope we _____

_____.

Bar-be-cues

The most fun I had at a picnic this summer
was at _____ on _____.
              (place)   (date)

People there: _____

_____

We ate _____.

My all-time *favorite* summer food is _____

_____. If I could, I would eat it ___

 times a week!

The picnic foods I like best are (circle):

chips   corn on the cob   watermelon

hot dogs   macaroni salad   potato salad

chicken   marshmallows   lemonade

pickles   hamburgers   other _____.

The things I love to do at picnics are _____

_____

_____.

TV Time

The TV show I like best is _____.

It's on _____ at _____.
(day)   (time)

My favorite episode was _____

_____.

My favorite summer rerun is _____

_____.

My favorite TV star is _____.

Other shows I like are _____

_____

_____.

If I could be the star of a TV show, I'd like to

be _____.

I can't wait to watch the new show _____

_____ this fall!

Winners!

My favorite baseball team is _____

_____, and _____

is my favorite player. He plays _____
(position)

_____.

I predict that _____

will win the World Series!

My favorite athletes are:

#1 _____

Sport _____

#2 _____

Sport _____

#3 _____

Sport _____

#4 _____

Sport _____

AUGUST

1

2

3

4

5

6

7

8

9

10

11

12

13

14

15

16

17

18

19

20

21

22

23

24

25

26

27

28

29

30

Moneybags

This summer I earned money by _____
_____.

I spent my hard-earned cash on _____
_____.

I'm saving my money for _____
_____

If I won $1,000 this summer I'd _____
_____
_____.

This Summer's Best

Beach _____

Pool _____

Amusement Park _____

Zoo _____

Museum _____

Party _____

Friend _____

Restaurant _____

Trip _____

Picnic _____

Sport _____

Fireworks _____

Ice Cream _____

Outfit _____

Back to School

School starts _____.

I go to _____ School. I'll be in

the _____ grade and my teacher will be

_____.

The back-to-school clothes I got for this year

are _____.

Supplies I got for school are _____

_____.

The friends I haven't seen since vacation

are _____.

This year in school I will try to _____

_____.

I'm looking forward to school because _____

_____.

Good-bye summer . . . HELLO SCHOOL!

SEPTEMBER

1

2

3

4

5

6

7

8

9

**Paste
Photo
Here**

A picture of me this summer.

Taken _____
(date)

at _____.
(place)